G4

ALSO BY

ROBERT HILLYER

RIVERHEAD
A NOVEL
(*1932*)

THE COLLECTED VERSE OF
ROBERT HILLYER
(*1933*)

These are Borzoi Books, published by
ALFRED A. KNOPF

A LETTER TO
ROBERT FROST

A LETTER TO
ROBERT FROST

AND OTHERS

BY

ROBERT HILLYER

NEW YORK & LONDON

ALFRED · A · KNOPF

1937

9095.

TO

JAMES BUELL MUNN

SPIRITUAL PATRON

OF THE ART OF POETRY

NOTE

Letter Number I, Letter Number II, Letter Number III, and Letter Number VI originally appeared in the *Atlantic Monthly;* Letter Number IV in the *Forum;* and Letter Number V in the *Saturday Review of Literature.* Grateful acknowledgment is made to the editors of these publications for permission to reprint.

Letter Number I was delivered before the chapter of Phi Beta Kappa at Columbia University in June, 1936; Letter Number III was delivered before the chapter of Phi Beta Kappa at Harvard University for the Tercentenary exercises in September, 1936.

With one exception, the poems are arranged in the order of their composition.

R. S. H.

CONTENTS

A LETTER TO
ROBERT FROST

A LETTER TO
ROBERT FROST

Our friendship, Robert, firm through twenty years,
Dares not commend these couplets to your ears:
How celebrate a thing so rich and strange—
Two poets whose affection does not change;
Immune to all the perils Nature sends,
World war and revolution and kind friends.
Something there is that doesn't love a wall;
Your apples and my pines knew none at all,
But grow together in that ghostly lot
Where your Vermont meets my Connecticut.
Ours is a startling friendship, because art,
Mother of quarrels who tears friends apart,
Has bound us ever closer, mind and heart.

Before the War, among those days that seem
Bathed in the slanting afterglow of dream,
Were happy autumn hours when you and I
Walked down that street still bright in memory.
I was a boy apprenticed to my rhymes,
Your fame already rose above our times,
Your shadow walking tall, my shorter gait,—
Both taller now, the difference as great.

Of wisdom I learned much, an artist's creed
Of work the flower, and worldly fame the weed;
I have forgotten phrases; it remains
As part of me, it courses in my veins.
From many conversations I remember
One on a windy day in late November.
The sly recluse of Amherst in those times
Moved me, in spite of questionable rhymes.
We talked of women poets, nothing else,
From Sappho to our friend at Sevenels.
"Miss Dickinson is best!" You shook your head.
"Perhaps a genius, but mad," you said.
Alas for Emily, alas for me,
That now I go much further than agree:
Once irresistible, now merely coy,
Her whims, her verbal airs and graces cloy.
Taste changes. Candid Louis Untermeyer
Consigns his past editions to the fire;
His new anthology, refined and thrifty,
Builds up some poets and dismisses fifty.
And every poet spared, as is but human,
Remarks upon his critical acumen.

Ah, could we know what vogue will be tomorrow,
What plumes of Paradise our pens could borrow!
Or to the Communistic muse entrust

Our sparrow feathers ruffling in the dust.
You bid me name no names, so I shall heed
By using cypher he who runs may read.
In short, I note the vogue no longer smiles
On one un-Briton in the British Isles;
Nor heeds from Italy that "wandering voice"
Whose absence should make Idaho rejoice.
Ah, sir, commend me to your quiet wit
That smiles at fraud and so dismembers it.
These twenty years the precious frauds I've seen
Relieved themselves of gall—and me of spleen.
You with relentless patience watch them go,
My rage prolongs their stay a week or so.

Yet not alone among the modern names
Does Fashion choose; she rummages in Fame's.
One poet to be praised—and sometimes read—
She chooses, and the rest are safely dead.
One must be sacrificed if one is praised,
As Crashaw mounts, Shelley must be abased.
With what astonishment we witnessed Donne,
A poet we have always counted on,
Whisked from his niche among the second shelves
And placed with Chaucer, Shakespeare,—and our-
    selves!
While Blake departs, abandoned by the vogue,

To Beulah-land, where Reason is the rogue;
And Hopkins, Fashion's choice to follow Donne,
Rattling his rusty iambs, climbs the sun.
Blest be thy name, O Vogue, that canst embalm
A minor poet with a potted palm;
Make me immortal in thy exegesis,—
Or failing that, at least a Doctor's thesis.

Yet, Robert, through the charlatans who swarm
Like blowing gnats before the social storm,
The stout immortals stand in this our time,
With manners, morals, metres,—even rhyme.
Not every age can triumph over death
In the bright train of Queen Elizabeth,
And our ingenious and cynic age
Has not quite lost the better heritage.
Take Robert Bridges, laureate forever,
Calm as the sea and flowing as a river,
Who knew his source and end, but also knew
The homely country he meandered through;
Who, when we thought his broadening current
    spent,
Flung high that sun-capped wave, his testament,
The *Testament of Beauty*. Of the few
Titles he gave his poems, all are true.
And Robinson, what other age but this

Has bred so classic an antithesis:
Mild in his manner, mocking in his eye,
Bold in appraisal, and in statement shy,
He knew all men,—the man against the sky.
And urbane Santayana, who alone
Among philosophers still seeks their Stone;
Whose irony, in golden prose alloyed
With doubt, yet yields not to the acid Freud;
Who after years of rightful fame defrauded,
Wrote one bad book at last,—and all applauded.

If gold get rusty, what shall iron do?
If poets, prophets, critics, are untrue
Why blame the statesmen, who in turn reflect
On dusty mirrors the uncircumspect?
When poets laugh at metres, with applause,
Why punish citizens who laugh at laws?
All follies regimented are akin—
Free verse and Bolshevism and bad gin.
Surely a subtle spring, in flow or drought,
Waters one age or burns another out.
When worlds go mad, all things go mad together,
Nations, philosophers, the arts, the weather.
Beholding war, Nature, who brooks no rival
In blind destruction, threatens Man's survival.
While underground he plants his dynamite,

She answers with an earthquake overnight.
While from ingenious wings his bombs rain down,
She rips the clouds apart, and cities drown.
Machine guns clatter, but her ticking worm
Of death bombards his armies with a germ.
Nor can the propaganda of slow doubt
That one by one puts all Faith's candles out
Find Nature unprepared; her insect ranks
For Man's destructive unbelief give thanks.
The ant, the termite, and their brotherhood
Wait busily, as all good soviets should,
To crack his concrete and to gnaw his wood,
And after war and storm have done their worst,
To view the last man, as they viewed the first.

From such dark thoughts only Dark Ages come;
I see not yet the end of Christendom;—
And if an end? In cloistered minds like yours
The classic wisdom of the past endures;
The ancient learning from the ancient guilt
Survives, and from slim chances worlds are built.
Black-armored barons, after Rome declined,
Warred on each other and on soul and mind;
Yet while they slept, cell after lonely cell,
Nearsighted eyes bent to the pliant quill.
The barons' mail adorns Park Avenue,

Quite spurious;—the words remain as true
As when, frail thread amid a mad sword-dance,
They led men to the sunlit Renaissance.
The things that make outlive the things that mar,
Rome and Byzantium crashed,—but here we are;
And even the dark spectre of dark ages
Calls forth old warriors who shame our sages:
Which would you choose, to put it in a word,—
To die with Arthur? or to live with Ford?

Men are as cells within a mighty brain
Swept with one thought of happiness or pain;
Thus when the Thinker gazed beyond all time
Egypt and China blossomed at their prime,
Both worshipers of beauty and of peace.
That mood resolved. He meditated Greece,
Whose culture, wedded to the arts of war,
Brought beauty forth and slew the thing it bore.
Less fortunate we who brought forth the machine
And dare not slay it, lest the truth be seen
That we, now helplessly identified
With the machine, would perish if it died.
We watch each other, our fates intertwined:
It feeds us canned goods and we feed it mind;
It kills us and then calls us from the grave
With new machines, lest it should lack a slave.

In war, where no one wins but the machine,
I pondered as I brought the wounded in:
Of these three choices—death, deformity,
Or patched for war again, who would not die?
And now the final triumph: the star actor
In *Steel: a Tragedy,* makes God a tractor.
Yet let us still believe, in thinking deeper,
These are but twitchings of a troubled Sleeper
In whom the nightmare rages, and who can
To-morrow dream the incredible—a Man.

Why, Robert, look! it's after midnight. Always
At this hour I hear stirrings in the hallways.
You would not mind. If I recall aright
You and Miss Lowell would converse all night,
Seldom agreeing, always the best friends
That poetry can shape to different ends;
Myself, too sleepy then as now, would run
To catch the last car back at half-past one.
Heigh-ho, I've seen worse things than morbid youth
Inscribes in his dark diary. The truth
Remains that my few perfect moments seem
Eternal, and the bad ones but a dream.
Like Johnson's friend, I woo philosophy,
But cheerfulness creeps in in spite of me.
So does the spirit sift a life away

Into its best, preparing for the day
When, from its golden nucleus, shall rise
That happy part attuned to happier skies.

But happier skies? That phrase is fustian stuff,—
This green Connecticut is good enough;
My shining acres and the house I built,
All mine, all earned, all mortgaged to the hilt.
If I may make some changes here and there
When halos play on my unhallowed hair,
New England winters well might be curtailed—
In May it snowed, and in July it hailed.
Rosebugs should all be banished, and with those
The people who see rosebugs on the rose.
And yet I shrink from this celestial boom,
Lest, with improvements, also I assume
Responsibility for things in bloom.
I might forget wax flowers of huckleberry,
I might leave out the fragrance of wild cherry;
In short, I hopefully resign to God
The natural world. O that our statesmen would!

And so good night with lullabye, my friend,
Republics fall and even letters end,
And Horace at one elbow sings of home
Far more eternal than the hills of Rome;—

Caesar, in fact, must marvel, looking down,
To find an Ethiope in his Gallic crown.
And Gibbon, at my other elbow, gives
Wry testimony of what dies, what lives,—
A secret not to be imparted, but
Known to Vermont and to Connecticut:
New as to-morrow's dawn, old as the Nile,
In Nefertiti's tears and Shakespeare's smile,
And all so simple in an age of guile;
For Horace on his acres has no fears,
His empire grows through twenty hundred years.

Good night, I take unconscionable time
A-dying, but in rhymeless years a rhyme
Bids one converse beyond the crack of dawn,—
It now has cracked, and dew is on the lawn.
Since I write oftener than you, I vow
Another letter twenty years from now.

A LETTER TO
CHARLES TOWNSEND COPELAND

Charles, shall we haunt a while that minor Heaven,
Named, more than numbered, Hollis Hall Eleven;
Affright the freshmen, then in turn rejoice
Their ears with echoes of your tempered voice?
Unthinking, as I pass the place at night,
My gaze roves upward to observe your light,
And halts, bedazzled by electric streams
Where in my memory your lamp still gleams.
What a brave host your memory could call
To that dim lighted room in Hollis Hall.
I see the two lamps glowing on the shelves
And books that have become your other selves:
In glimmering ranks, their wit and wisdom spread,—
Friends of your heart, familiars of your head;
And—what to me was more important still—
Musicians of your voice in joinëd skill.
And then I see, as face by face appears—
Some kin to laughter, some aloof from tears—
Your young apprentices of other years.
Some, able to perform as well as learn,
From high entablatures of fame return;
More, though of equal promise, doomed to lose
Their gift in banking, salesmanship, or booze.

Yet even these, when bank directors meet,
Hear echoes from the "Ballad of the Fleet."
Or suddenly, through smoke and doubtful stories,
Remember that the Azores are Azorës.
Or quote, and quote it as their own, your line:
To eat is human, to digest divine.
And others come, without reproach or stain,
The ever young, who died—and died in vain;
Yet proved, while shaming Europe's vile pretence,
America's high heart, and innocence.

It is a common error to behold
In every previous age the age of gold.
When Norton quit his Chair—which was a throne—
Young Wendell knew that Harvard's day was done.
He mourned the passing of all learned grace
Of which he found not one remaining trace
Among his colleagues,—and his colleagues were
Young Briggs, young Kittredge, and young Cope-
    land, sir,
And many others whose retirement left
My later age of learned grace bereft.
Had I not Wendell's letter as a warning,
I too should don epistolary mourning;
For, of a truth, the Harvard that I knew
Needed no distance to enchant the view.

And memory, that sometimes may enhance,
But dims the vistas of my backward glance.

As dusk comes on, I almost hope to meet
Dean Briggs once more in the familiar street,
His head thrown back, his amiable walk
Timed equally to progress or to talk.
I, whom life changes with its every whim
Remember now his steadfastness. In him
Was a perfection, an unworldly grace,
Life could not mar and death can not efface.
I know the wrinkled smile, the kindly eyes,
Keen with a wit both humorous and wise,—
These I remember, and remembering, see
The Dean walk home toward immortality.
The Dean walks home, his cheerful task complete;
He walks at dusk down the familiar street,
Stopping to share some story with a friend,
Or murmur words of counsel. At the end
He pauses for a moment, and with shy
Farewell looks back, looks back and says Goodbye;
Then rounds the corner of his shining days,
His smile at parting bright through April haze.

By whom shall brilliant minds—and dull—be fired
(In double sense) now Kittredge has retired?

The *Beowulf* was no book on a shelf,
There stood the veteran Beowulf himself!
The Viking beard, a sail; the nose, a prow;
Blue eyes the riding lights from here-and-now.
He'd cruise, head down, hands clasped behind his
    back,
With changing winds of thought in veering tack;
Then jibing suddenly full-face, stop short
And bring his cargo of ideas to port.
Daring the doubters, how he would expound
That day-long dive of Beowulf—undrowned.
Belief in this unscientific story
Was, to a science-hater, mandatory.
"They say the Middle Ages were priest-ridden,
That fantasy was taught, and fact forbidden.
This may be true, but how much more unpleasant
A world by science ridden, as at present.
I'd rather far be ridden, I insist,
By any priest than by a scientist."
A Beowulf in mien,—but I miscall
The scholar who is Shakespeare to them all.

No doubt when Adam delved and Evë span,
Wendell already was the gentleman,
The embodied form of that elusive term,
Its foibles clear, its virtues deep and firm.

New Englander, with British elegance,
The culture and the courtesy of France,
He claimed our so neglected right to use
The good of Europe, and the bad refuse.
The while his discourse edified his classes,
Their frightened gaze pursued his whirling glasses;
Taut on the string in shortening whorls they flew
Faster and faster as his interest grew,
Till on his forefinger completely wound,
They paused, then whirled the other way around.
And to this day, of Wendell I recall
A jeopardy, a voice with dying fall,
A ducal face, urbane beyond surprise,
And of all eyes I've seen, the saddest eyes.

It is the function of the truly great
To fix the letters on time's dimming slate.
Hence, kings make history we con by rote;
Republics are mere records of a vote.
Facts are forgotten soon, unless they can
Be attributes of a remembered man.
Subjects too often overweigh the thought,
The teacher matters more than what is taught.
And all, the theories and the facts must be
Shaped to their place in vast philosophy.
Bliss Perry gave me more than Tennyson,

And Spaulding, more than melody and tone;
Had I not studied Bonaparte's campaign
With Johnston, I had studied it in vain.
Music I courted, Greek philosophies,
The Parthenon, exclusive of the frieze,—
A furious medley, logic put to rout,
And not one item I could do without.
Painters of Florence, poets of Japan,
Course after course,—but more, man after man;
For fields of interest were not drawn so fine,—
I moved about, I did not toe the line.
Thus, Thaxter, the great botanist, with whom
I never took a course, yet brought to bloom
Far fairer plants than liverworts or palms,—
Two charming daughters and a taste for Brahms.
And Taussig, economics put aside,
In hospitable plenitude applied
The theory of supply and of demand
When freshman appetites got out of hand.
And Briggs, how did he teach? I can't conjecture;
Was it example, talk, or formal lecture?

From minds like these how rich has been my yield,
However foreign may have seemed the field.
The human mind, of various fibres blent,
Draws from variety its nourishment,

Lest it be shrunken inly to a very
Anatomy of mental dysentery.
Much narrow learning is but hocus-pocus
Compared with wars in Spain or the first crocus;
For men, if education be not vain,
Must rise with crocuses, not fall with Spain.
All needful knowledge to the mind impart,
But better, understanding to the heart.
The little learning that is dangerous, may
Be having all our learning go one way.
Toilers by midnight oil will scarce be drawn
To meet the sun upon the upland lawn,
And those who hunt mere sources, always bungle
Through literature itself, which is their jungle.
I know an unknown Restoration drama,
And whence, verbatim, Emerson got "Brahma,"
Whence Pope his "taste not the Pierian spring,"
And I can guess what song the sirens sing.
These learned contributions must, however,
Await some far more serious endeavour,—
Till in the *Modern Language Notes* they cumber
Page after page of the Greek Kalends' number.

Charles, you're not listening, and I shall creep
Tiptoe away down corridors of sleep.
I shall go home, and for a penance, mark

A score of themes at random in the dark.
I shall put out the street lamps as I go,
Wrap up the city in a hush of snow,
Turn off all motors, smooth the wind with grease,
Lest you be wakened and reread this piece.
Before your eyelids closed, I saw despair
Flow out and freeze to resignation there;
Bored by the poet, kindly to the friend,
And wishing both of them would make an end.
What! wide awake? "And watching, Bob. I hope
You are not practising to tread a rope.
Your exit would leave nothing to be said
For burying a man before he's dead.
'Tis not the man I'd pity, but the mourners
Mincing such circumvolutory corners.
This poem—so to speak—leaves me aghast
By your preoccupation with the past.
Why are the young so old? have they not learned
No chicken's ever to the egg returned?
Let's have no more of that.   Let's look ahead.
We can look back a long while when we're dead.
After us, not the deluge, but the sun.
All things must pass, and when good things are done,
It's time that something better were begun."

A LETTER TO
JAMES B. MUNN

Your learning, James, in classics and romance,
Sits lightlier than most men's ignorance.
It is yourself, an undivided part
Of you as man, not only mind but heart.
How often do I see in our profession
Learning a mere extraneous possession,
A self-sufficient mass of dates and sources
Roll'd round in academe's diurnal courses,
Where scholars prepare scholars, not for life
But gaudy footnotes and a threadbare wife,—
Keen eyes for errors in a worthless text,
But none at all for this world or the next.
Your modesty, that even tops your learning,
Forbids what I would say of you, so turning
Not, as I hope, from Ghibelline to Guelph,
I will discuss, as is the vogue, myself.

I fall between two stools—I can't say Chairs—
A bard too learn'd, a scholar in arrears.
The critical reviewers, week by week,
Damn poets who command their own technique.
Professor is a title that to them
Begins in laughter and concludes in phlegm.

A careful rhyme, a spondee nobly planned
Is academic, and the work unmanned.
Would that these critics lived in houses fashioned
By carpenters congenially impassioned.
I'd love to see the rooftree fall on . . . no,
The name is legion; let us leave it so.
But as a teacher I have equal luck,—
In ponds a chicken and on shore a duck.
My wretched memory, for all my pains,
Drops tons for every ounce that it retains;
Far wiser now, I have less factual knowledge
At forty-one than when I was in college.
With eyes astonished, I peruse the rant
My younger self delivered against Kant.
The *Critique of Pure Reason* was to me
Mere holiday from Greek philosophy.
The Greeks I can remember in due season,
But where now is the *Critique of Pure Reason?*
Alas, that educated men should find
Their memory not equal to their mind!
But since I have to choose, the lifeless fact
Must yield before the will to write and act.
Though I salute my past for what he knew
Let him return the bow for what I do;—
Thus to reverse, and much more truly say:
Si vieillesse savait, si ieunesse pouvait.

Yet there is recompense for knowing well
One language, if it be incomparable.
Disdainful, the Athenian would speak
No other language than his native Greek.
Now his provincial literature is prized
In every barbarous tongue that he despised.
The learned Roman, who knew Greek by heart,
Had twice the scholarship, and half the art.
The great Elizabethans' education
Thrived less on lore than on superb translation.
Our scholars, to whom every root is known,
Command all languages, except their own;
For confirmation, but consult the theses
That year by year bankrupt the college presses.

When poets go, grammarians arrive.
Is Virgil dead? Let commentators thrive.
The gift of tongues without the Holy Ghost
Is but a Babel, not a Pentecost.
Research in science may produce the answer
To love or wealth, to authorship or cancer;
Research in language? What is there to cure?
Some languages are dead and some endure,
Some fossil bones, some living literature.
Science in language is a game, designed
As rare Ben Jonson said, to break a mind;

One lives in words or knows them not at all
And weeps at the grammarian's funeral.
Romantic doctrine if you will, but who
Knowing his Gothic, knows his English too?

Mere English, mightiest tongue, whose cadences
Roar with the tides and murmur with the trees,
Since I hear living beauty, what care I
What tongues dared frame thy fearful symmetry?
I will not see thee petrified, my native
Language frozen to a fossil dative.
In short, dear James, by now you plainly see
I find no virtue in philology;
At best a sterile hobby, often worse,
The plumes, when language dies, upon its hearse.

Beside Illisus under the cool trees
Youth answered questions put by Socrates.
It does not matter what the questions were,
Suffice the youth and the philosopher.
Both, doubtless, would have thought it very odd
To trace the genitives in Hesiod;
Their works were intermingled with their days,
It was enough to know, not paraphrase.
Their voices reach me this calm afternoon
Through the bright air honeyed with ample June

More clearly than the meaningless confusion
That dominates the modern world's illusion.
Clearest of all, one question rouses me:
"Why have you lost the old simplicity
In life and learning, politics and art,
While wisdom, peace, and innocence depart?"

Though we who teach cry out against the mesh
Spread by the world, the Devil, and the flesh
To entrap the moneyed in material things
While we at lofty altitude spread wings,
Yet are we not materialists ourselves?
They build their mansions, we extend our shelves;
They flaunt possessions, we a weary text,
One-tenth original, nine-tenths indexed,
Both of us sharing in a common loss
Of life's essentials smothered by a gloss.

Now, James, I stop complaining, I will plan
An education to produce a man.
Make no mistake, I do not want this done,—
My limitations are the cornerstone.
Plato's *Republic* may have served some use
In manuscript, but not in Syracuse,
So let my dream Academy remain
A dream;—I'm sure I do not ask in vain.

First would I have my scholar learn the tongue
He never learned to speak when he was young;
Then would I have him read therein, but merely
In the great books, to understand them clearly.
At present, for no earthly good, we ask
A deadly and unnecessary task:
A knowledge of small names that time has taken
And put to bed—and whom we vainly waken.
O that our living literature could be
Our sustenance, not archaeology!
Time is the wisest judge, who folds away
The surplus of a too-abundant day.
My scholar shall be brilliantly forbidden
To dig old garbage from a kitchen midden;
Old it may be, and curious as old,
But I would have him dig for purest gold:
The text itself, no footnotes but his own,
And critics who let well enough alone.
Far better Alexandria in flames
Than buried beneath unimportant names;
And even Sappho, glory that was Greece's,
Lives best, I blasphemously think, in pieces.
Surely our sprite, who over Amherst hovered,
Would gain if no more poems were discovered.
That Chinese emperor who burned the books
Succumbed to madness shrewder than it looks;

The minor poets and the minor sages
Went up in smoke; the great shine down the ages.
The Harvard Library's ungainly porch
Has often made me hunger for a torch,
But this not more to simplify a lecture
Than to appease the Muse of architecture.

When music and sweet poetry agree,
Who would be thinking of a Ph.D.?
O who would ablauts bear, when Brahms's First
Is soon to be performed or but rehearsed?
My scholar must have music in his heart,
Bach and Beethoven, Schumann and Mozart,
Franck and Sibelius, and more like these,
Their works, if not their names, sweet symphonies.
Ah James, I missed my calling; I would turn
To that one art toward which the others yearn,—
But I observe my neighbour's cow, who leaves
Her fertile pasture for my barren sheaves.
The field next-door, the next-door art, will thus
Always attract the mildly covetous.
Yet some day I will play you the main theme
Of the immortal counterpoint I dream:
Clear melody in fugue and canon rises
On strings, with many structural surprises.
No letter, but a prelude, for your sake

I would compose beside this tranquil lake.
Its line should rise toward heaven until it broke
Half-way between the sky and the great oak;
Then waver, like a flock of homing birds,
In slow descending flights of minor thirds.
Music alone can set the spirit free
From the dark past and darker things to be.
I'd live for ever in an atmosphere
Of high harmonics where all tones are clear.
Could Man be judged by music, then the Lord
Would quench the angel of the flaming sword.
Alas, the final tones so soon disperse
Their echoes through the empty universe,
And hearers, weak from following Beethoven,
Relax with Gershwin, Herbert, and de Koven.

But to return to Polyhymnia,
And incidentally to my student. Ah,
Where is the creature? Nay, but is that he?
A saxophone is nuzzling on his knee!
His eyes pop out, his bellied cheeks expand,
His foot taps "Alexander's Ragtime Band."
Ungraceful and unpardonable wretch!
Was it for you my eager pen would sketch
A new, a sensible curriculum?
Burst with your panpipes! and we'll both be dumb.

I was about to urge philosophy,
Especially the Greek, I was to be
Your godfather in recommending Faith
To you, fit godson for a Sigmund Spaeth!
Of history and time I was to tell,
Things visible and things invisible,
But what to you are echoes from Nicæa,
Who never prayed nor cherished an idea?
And what have you to gain from education,
Blown bellows for unceasing syncopation?
Learning and life are too far wrenched apart,
I can not reconcile, for all my art,
Studies that go one way and life another,
Tastes that demoralize, and tests that smother.

James, what is this I find? an angry scowl
Sits on my brow like a Palladian owl!
Let me erase it, lest it should transform
The soft horizon with a thunder storm.
I would you were beside me now, to share
The sound of falling water, the sweet air.
Under the yew a vacant easy chair
Awaits your coming; and long-planted seeds
Begin to bloom amid the encircling weeds.
I bade my student an abrupt adieu
But find it harder to take leave of you.

May we not some day have a mild carouse
In Pontefract instead of Warren House?
The distance nothing,—in two hours' time
Another land where that word's but a rhyme.
Would I were Marvell, then you could not harden
Your heart against a visit to my garden.
I'd write those happy lines about the green
Annihilation, and you'd soon be seen
Hatless and coatless, bootless,—well, my soul!
He's in the lake with nothing on at all!
To sink, to swim, that is the only question:
Thus ends my treatise on—was it digestion?
Farewell, and yours sincerely, and yours ever,
The time has come for the initial shiver.
When into lakes, as into life, we dive,
We're fortunate if we come up alive.

A LETTER TO
PEYTON RANDOLPH CAMPBELL
[KILLED IN ACTION, 1918]

You'll laugh, dear Randolph, to perceive that Satan
Has moved me to include the name of Peyton.
Well I remember the unreasoning shame
Your boyhood felt for that illustrious name.
I felt it for my middle name. We knew
How to annoy each other, as friends do.
"Peyton!" I'd shout, and "Silliman!" you'd cry,—
The fight was on, and fists began to fly.
I never walk down a suburban street
In autumn, when the blazing maples meet
Far overhead in tunneled radiance,
Without an unpremeditated glance
To find two little boys so hard at play
All life seems but an autumn holiday,
When the ripe grapes hang heavy from the vine
In shadowy arbours fragrant as old wine.

Life did not grant you much in days thereafter
But disappointments and the gift of laughter.
Some power must be, who accurately judges
To the last ounce how much the human drudges
Can carry, and then piles upon their backs,

Up to the breaking point, the futile packs.
You were a good man and you did good things;
And your reward? The shell, how shrill it sings!

A dubious reward, perhaps the best
For one who, finding evil, could not rest.
Evil enough there is, my lad, to keep
For ever aliens, your soul and sleep.
Perhaps more happy thus at twenty-four
To die, than struggle in this darker war,—
The spirit caught between the lines, the zero
Hour at dawn, where no dawn is, nor hero.
Those countries, our allies—or so we thought,
Have proved as evil as the one we fought;
All Europe, cheats and cravens to a man,
Except the honest Scandinavian.

This drifting world needs men like you to man it;
I chide you for abandoning the planet.
Surely you might have dodged the shell, or better,
Persuaded with a diplomatic letter,
As others did, that you were valuable
Behind the lines, but not before a shell.
Alas, you yielded to your ruling vice,
A shameful lack of guile or cowardice.

You who were young, knew not when you were
    hurled
So suddenly, so brutally, from the world,
That you died vainly, and the truth you died for
Was but a sham that Englishmen had lied for.
You gave your life, as fine as it was short,
Not to your country, but the *Bryce Report,*
A document so void for sacrifice
It even, when the war was done, shocked Bryce,
Whose conscience bade him clear it off the slate,
A handsome disavowal—rather late.
But grown mature in spirit you may scan
Quite without bitterness that larger plan,
Where, nobly if mistakenly intended,
Your gift shall live when the last war has ended,—
A date that coincides, I greatly fear,
With Man's departure from this earthly sphere.

How shall we reach the dead? I can persuade
Your voice to echo back, or call your shade
Before me, as with wonted eagerness,
You bring me proof sheets from your printing press.
"Proofreader's error!" you would smile. I knew
Your spelling, though the best that you could do,
Disclosed that printer was proofreader, too.
I can recall the little boy of four,

Or the young sergeant in the ancient war;
The adolescent scholar, the athlete,
His winged spirit swift in winged feet.
All those were you; now they are part of me.
My thoughts are not your immortality;
Thoughts never have been, they can never be.
Nor on this quiet morning do I look
For hints of you in wind or flower or brook.
Nature has business of her own—to live!
She has no immortality to give,
But feeds on life and death alike, nor cares
If it be Shakespeare or a flea she bears.
The page is blank where once she wrote preamble
To the undying *Life of Randolph Campbell,*—
Proofreader to himself, and master printer
Misspelling life for death and spring for winter.

How shall we reach the dead? Shall it be thus:
A darkened room to awe the credulous,
A spiritistic circle, hand in hand,
A-sweat with visions of the Promised Land,
Whence, from the jasper walls and golden sheen
And gallant walks continually green,
Spirits return to thump a tambourine?
Our Lady sings *Magnificat* with tones
Surpassing sweet. These whistle "Casey Jones";

And, when consulted on immortal things,
Divulge locations of lost wedding rings.
The medium snores; the fit's upon her now,
One hand moves slumberously to her brow,
And thus distracts the faithful from pursuing
With their attention, what the other's doing.
It, from beneath her negligée, produces
An apparatus deft for sundry uses.
A handsome fraud it is. It puzzled me,
Yet I confess that my credulity
Has often made me but a laughing-stock
To friends who thrive as friends when they can mock.
I never in my wildest moments thought
These were our dead. Wisely the Church has taught
That certain imps or elementals see
This chance for mischief,—so it seemed to me;
Imps aided, I now add, by limbs elastic,
Quite fleshly and incredibly gymnastic.
Far better the mute ashes of the Stoic
Than imbecilities so unheroic.
I can not hear the saints in sweet accord
Inscribing gibberish on a ouija board,
Nor flights of angels bearing to its rest
A table battered in a tipping test.
The undertakers at the funeral, fill
The open grave, then dwindle to a bill;

The medium, inspired by her "control"
Extorts fresh payment from a bogus soul,
Composed, if the survivors only knew it,
Of Gloucester glue and sleight of hand and suet.

How shall we reach the dead? Are they reborn,
Bewildered mortals in a second morn?
Reincarnations whom the years discover
Unweaving and reweaving their lives over?
Disarmed of all experience, to make
The same small triumph and the same mistake,
Repeated through the ages, till they press
On to Nirvana, crowned with Nothingness?
Better a phantom universe than none,—
Anything, anything, but oblivion.
Let others put two mirrors face to face
To see themselves reflected beyond space;
In space and time wherein I dwell at present,
I use one glass and find it not unpleasant;
Except that time, fast greying on my brow,
Bids me enlist in the Eternal Now.
Reincarnation of the soul! of all
The theories, thou art the most logical,
A spiritual Darwinism, blest
By the huge shadow of Mount Everest.
From life to life ascending, spirits fashion

A gradual release from earthly passion,
Until a loincloth is their total clothing,
And that whisked off,—Nirvana! There is nothing.

Buddha, in whom all crude mutations cease,
Looms from the lotus, smilingly at peace;
The lotus flower at rest, the wheel of time
Stopped like a heartbeat from too high a climb.
Beneath that bending head, that dreamless face,
Time dies in an infinity of space.

Ah, vista of reincarnated lives,
Where no one less than king or queen survives,
How thou hast recompensed for lost romances
Old maids and wives in modest circumstances!
'Tis Cleopatra risen from the tomb
Who shines the pots and brandishes the broom.
I never yet have met the Christian slave,
But Queens of Babylon denude the grave.
Back from the past reënter, self-appointed,
More monarchs than the Lord could have anointed.

How shall we reach the dead?—Why should we
      reach them?
Just what have they to gain, or we to teach them?
Love is a bridge they may, perhaps, recross,—

Unwise, to drop in for an afterloss.
I can define the *here;* the *there* remains
A mystery unsolved, for all my pains.
The wise man, like Columbus, still prefers
His course unblurred by bad cartographers.
Sail west. Though India was your intent,
Accept, O valiant, a new continent,
Uncharted in the logic of the mind,
A faith not to be named, much less defined.
Prove it? Subjected to the earthly laws
Of reason and equation, faith withdraws.
Transcendent, it is an experience
Beyond the net of thought, the thrill of sense.
At intervals unheralded, it flows
Through all the being, and that moment knows
Eternity; its altitude goes out
Beyond all ages in an age of doubt.
Nor can belief by unbelief be bribed
To prove what can not even be described.
Far better so; we can not pass our days
Beneath the sun, blind from the fiercer blaze.
I have no patience with the so-called mystic
Who lives on crusts and symbols kabbalistic.
Yeats and his comrades in the Celtic dusk
Throw out the kernel and enjoy the husk.
The real conviction is austere and sharp;

A clear, high tone,—not an Aeolian harp.
It dies, but let us not in depths of night
Ever deny that we have seen the light.
Psychology, beware! this is, of all
Our human states, the least hysterical;
A quiet, where we make deliberate choices
Quite unaccompanied by phantom voices.

Voltaire wrote, "One world at a time!" For once
I'm in accord with that sagacious dunce;
Yet I will not permit one world to smother
My absolute conviction of another.
Perhaps the Universe, like Nature, seeds
Its garden many times beyond its needs.
It may be, as the wise Egyptians taught,
Some are immortal seed, and some are not.
Spirits have privilege of suicide;
I've seen them die before the body died,
The soul cut off from the immortal air
By lust or greed or cynical despair.

But in your heart, no evil thing could enter.
Your being, Randolph, from its radiant centre,
Glowed through misfortunes beyond your control
That would have darkened a less manly soul.
I hesitate. In all our mortal days

We never once exchanged a word of praise!
How shy is youth, how strangely reticent,
So long withholding words we always meant!
But take them now, old friend; translate them better
Than earthly phrase affords this random letter.
Now through the mist, the Sunday morning bell
Rings murmurously over Woodstock hill.
Sanctus! the bell intones, and *Sanctus!* I
Deep in my wayward spirit make reply.
Therefore with angels and archangels, all
The company of Heaven lift the pall
From the dead past, and like a sudden shout
Across deep valleys, the bright sun comes out.
Forgive me, Randolph, for old friendship's sake,
That I sit quietly beside the lake.
I smell the incense of the risen morn,
I see the rose crowning the conquered thorn,
And I believe, though absent from the Mass,
That glories were, that glories come to pass.

Peyton! farewell from Silliman! God knows,
I'd love to see you though we came to blows.

A LETTER TO
BERNARD DEVOTO

Time brings us, Benny, to our middle years,
Not unattuned to life or our careers.
In tasks that after war seemed merely play,
We hastened to make up for war's delay.
Youth, overstimulated by reverses,
Wrings blessings, sometimes, from expected curses,
As mediaeval necromancers bent them
And flung them back against the ones who sent them.
My memory works strangely like a sieve,
I drop the bad, the happy I relive;
A fatal disposition for to-day,
When memories should work the other way.
Thus, if I think of war, my backward glance
Shows me Dos Passos in a frenzied dance,
Unwonted ecstasy upon his face
As shrapnel tears his raincoat into lace.
He was not in the coat,—had that been true,
Three soldiers would have been reduced to two.
Good luck, in so unheralded a stroke,
By incongruity becomes a joke,
Something to dance to, though great nations ebb,
And Burberrys are raveled to a web.

But why do shell-shocked veterans increase
Among the children of unbroken peace,
Whose pocketbooks are lined with golden fleece?
When our hope faltered, discipline achieved
Through will what hope would never have be-
    lieved.
How much less fortunate a generation
Where doubt is dogma, faith a speculation.
Almost I'd choose the boredom and the wrath
Of war to war's neurotic aftermath.
Do not misread me, I would not prescribe
An evil that demands a diatribe,
But why should so much poetry and fiction
Be Pollyanna in reverse direction,—
Alike by sentimentalism fired,
She wafted skyward, they completely mired.
False hope or false despair, a bogus passion,
Dependent on the maunderings of fashion.

Art is so long and human life so short,
In hurried years young novelists resort
To sweet publicity, that freely offers
Headlines to vanity and cheques to coffers.
They snatch at tribute due a deathless name,
The fruits, without the patient growth, of fame;
Like millionaires, impatient of slow Nature,

Who transplant trees grown to their fullest stature,
Till bankruptcy and weather overwhelm
Both pocketbook and unancestral elm.
As fast as pen can trot, young writers build
Volumes, compact of words, but unfulfilled;
The sound and fury so intense, that often
The Muse's corpse is justled from her coffin,
Where she lay dying in a rattling hearse
Driven by Faulkner, Wolfe, and even worse.
When tragedy descends from Court to hovel
Fit men make no fit subject for a novel,
But only monsters whose creators, even,
Confuse them, and John reappears as Stephen,—
A trifling slip, no doubt, it yet suffices
To limit the consistency to vices;
Except that one must ponder if the style
Or matter is consistently more vile.
They look not to the distant mountains. Death
Is in their eyes and madness in their breath.
Around, in never-lifting vapours curled
Lie all the fetid miseries of the world;
While, as through city snow, on muffled feet
The baffled spirits move in long retreat,
Passing, repassing; slantwise through the haze
Their bloodshot eyes in dying sockets glaze.
If one were recognizable as man

We'd tremble, as perhaps their authors can,
But Ariel's as true as Caliban.

Add to these self-tormented symbolists,
Seas of red ink, savannas of clenched fists.
The propagandist boys, who boys remain
Though fifty acid years corrode the drain,
Their hero, Marx; their laureate, Hart Crane.
A combination one might find emetic
Of impure politics and false aesthetic,
But for the common bond of failure; this
Being the pass to apotheosis.
With what assurance our eccentric neighbour
Ascribes to luck what we have won with labour;
He cut his coupons, while we earned our bread;
Our day of work half done, he rose from bed
To vent his spite against a social order
That welcomed him as guest, and me as boarder.
To such, all work is tyranny, encrusted
With complications for the maladjusted,
For from whatever quarter blows the wind,
It stings the nose of the undisciplined.

Perhaps the social order should be ended,
But wherein has the English tongue offended?
The proletarians must think it has
Some vague connection with Czar Nicholas.

Good syntax and the niceties of style
Like weary kulaks wander in exile;
Harvests of English usage are laid waste
By vast coöperatives of bad taste.
Averse to discipline in any field,
They talk, we heed; they write, they are revealed.
Let phrases keener than these couplets smite them;
They can not answer, for they can not write them.

"O if Rome had one neck! and I a sword!"
Cried Rome's exasperated overlord.
We view the literary mobs, and ah,
Who would not echo wise Caligula?
Is there no city where they meet, or rather
Some single room where all the schools foregather?
The Communist, the psychoanalytic,
The aesthete, and the defutated critic?
Of course there is! A gross expatriate
Has condescended to a lecture date,—
Her bank account commanding,—and she sits
Enthroned at cocktail parties in the Ritz;
A mammoth idol round whose granite flanks
The writers gyrate in unsteady ranks.

There by the wall a maiden poet stands,
Her gestures undulant on languid hands;

Each finger nail a crimson petal, seen
Through a pale garnishing of nicotine.
Her draperies, like downward vapour, tremble,
As one by one her courtiers assemble.
Her wistful eyes, now gazing far, report
Her rival's shoulder strap and smaller court.
She smiles,—it is the same ecstatic smile
That graced the sacred cats along the Nile.
Now budding authors flutter to full bloom,
Spying an editor across the room.
Some strike an attitude, and some advance
In Marathons if not in Pyrrhic dance.
As in Ravel's familiar piece, crescendos
Pound till they shake the glass in all the win-
    dows,
So, like the drums, the rhythmic cocktails urge
Fortissimos to even fiercer surge;
Voice mounting voice until amid the riot
Stravinsky's *Rites of Spring* would seem too quiet.
A novelist, whose enviable position
Explains, but does not warrant, his condition,
Reiterantly through the medley yelps:
"You'll sell ten thousand if you're praised by
    Phelps!"
A statement we must doubt, until we hear
That thirty billion books are sold a year.

But silence! Like the weary horn that wound
Through Roncevaux its melancholy sound,
When the dull evening fell, and Roland, dy-
    ing,
Heard from the crags only the echoes crying;
And Nature, pitiful for once, was still
In sudden hush upon the darkening hill,—
Silence! the Columnist is on the sill!
An ample Muse, she pauses for effect,
With sequins and synthetic pearls bedecked.
Upon her shoulder ferns and one white lily
Recall the Venus in a Botticelli;—
Not sea-born Venus, but that later era,
The pregnant Venus of the Primavera.
She enters with triumphant condescension
Exuding promises of Sunday mention.
Impishly coy, grandiloquent with power,
She bids await the inevitable hour
When printer's ink shall scatter her largesse
On writers who have won their own success.
Camp-follower of literature, acclaimed
By all the nameless longing to be named,
She is our hope, our symbol! And is this
The end of literature? I fear it is.
That flaccid neck is all we hate of Rome,—
Your sword, Caligula. My lord, strike home!

Well, Benny, if 'twere said, 'twere better said;
My pen grows dull; besides, the wench is dead.
I sit an exile now, in far Vermont
Scolding of this and that as is my wont.
Have not New Englanders sufficient taste
Of winter that in summer months they waste
Their August chance of basking like a lizard
By traveling north to meet an August blizzard?
You, as Vermonter, find these lines effete,
But I am homesick for a touch of heat.
Yet think me not a malcontent, I bask
In sunlight strong as anyone could ask:
The warmth of eager minds, the affluent reach
Of those who learn far better than I teach.
Here in this amiable school one finds
That the ambition of most human minds
When balanced normally, is to bespeak
Not chaos but a pattern for technique;
And widening my gaze, I guess that Man
Provided with a plan would fill the plan.

In this unhurried universe, how clear
The metred stars ascending, tier on tier,
Wake amid muted chaos, sounds that change
To light in that immeasurable range,
While through the answering valleys, spark on spark,

The lamps of men order their little dark.
From unseen atoms to blind space beyond
All in unbroken balance correspond.
Drive chaos back! Unutterably conveyed,
That theme is life, and that must be obeyed;
Though meteors break loose, and self-expression
Affords indulgent chances for confession.
All things but chaos balance in design,
Planets in orbit, words in written line;
Yet chaos, mirrored in unruly hearts,
Though shunned in Heaven, shadows earthly arts.
Let passion clamour, reason still refers
For evidence to atoms and the stars.

Well, sir, without intent I seem to be
Your mentor in a new astrology.
Be Sagittarius, whose keen-eyed arrows
Fly deftly past the swans and hit the sparrows.
You'll be beslavered and you'll be accused,
Praised to your face, behind your back, abused;
The smiler with the knife beneath his candy
Will have his cards of introduction handy.
But happily you know. Ah, good my friend,
Bid common sense return and nonsense end.

A LETTER TO
MY SON

Between us, Stanley, we must bridge a span
Perhaps the broadest in the life of Man.
McKinley and Victoria, familiar
As household gods when I was the young Hillyer,
To ashes and to legend have gone down,—
And Mickey Mouse has ousted Buster Brown.
In green suburban streets I played at ease,
Untroubled by the passing carriages,
Save when some dowager, averse to ball,
Scowled at us, brandishing her parasol,
Yet left (because of Grandmother) unspoken
Her thoughts of stolen grapes and windows broken.
Alas! though Mrs. Howe has been entombed
Some thirty years, my palate was foredoomed
Never again to taste such provender
As that forbidden fruit I stole from her.
I smell the arbours now, I see the lawn
Yellow with leaves like flakes of shattered dawn;
I smell the bonfire smoke, I smell the grapes;
But the October flavour still escapes.
I've planted twenty vineyards since that time
To catch the mixture of sweet juice and rime,
And not one grape, however cool and swollen,

Renews the ecstasy of those I've stolen.
Pray do not in your after years, reread
As "theft the simplest method to succeed"
These casual lines. Our family does not mix
In banking, surgery, or politics.

It was a safe time, when all's said and done;
Backyards were big, streets open to the sun.
But sometimes, as if fashioned to disturb,
A horseless carriage pushed us to the curb;
Where teetering with fury, in full force
We shouted to the driver, "Get a horse!"
An incantation powerful enough
To stop the motor with expiring cough;
Whereat the driver, cursing as we jeered,
Beneath the underpinning disappeared.
O for the wisdom of those saucy boys
Who rightly guessed a danger in such toys,
Now toys no longer. With inverted rôles,
Motors have made mere playthings of men's souls.
Not war, not plague, not any ill you mention
Has crushed mankind like this obscene invention;
All life resolves, in leisure or in toil,
To the production or misuse of oil.
Man's body flung full speed straight up the hill
Mounts with a nervous lift; his mind is nil.

Free in the air he skims, the while his spirit
Dives down to every ill that brutes inherit.
Let others praise inventiveness; I know
That where wings go there also bombs can go.
In short, dear son, my aging nervous centres
Quiver with indignation at inventors;
But you, no doubt, will find it commonplace
To speed through time and hurtle into space:
Two elements that bend to Berkeley's dream
By being something less than what they seem.
But though speedometers burn up with speed,
And clocks whirl madly at a moment's need,
Eternity awaits. That does not heed.

Yet I am not so much a misanthrope
As to conceive my past a future hope.
Things change, and that is well, and I am weary
Of the past gilded, and the future dreary.
Your childhood is just so much happier
As I am wiser than my parents were;—
Not to contemn them, but if sudden change
In common life swirls in so great a range,
Surely a loving and astute perspective
Ignores what once inspired a long invective.
I have not taught you that the fiends stand ready
To pierce with red-hot pitchforks, Mrs. Eddy;

Nor that the tentacles of furtive Spain
Groped to Havana and blew up the *Maine;*
Nor that the Unitarians and Jews
Have invitations they can not refuse
To an unending carnival of fire
Where all non-Trinitarians perspire.
The High Church and the Low Church still may vie;
You do not know it, Stanley,—nor do I.
Please God, that you are so much the more near Him
For hearing fewer things that don't endear Him.

Yet with it all, I would not seem to mock
My minute spent on the ancestral clock.
It was a nervous time, and I prefer
To split the seconds where they did not err.
Music I had and Christmas trees and books,
A sound physique and tolerable looks;
And something more, of undetermined cause,
That always irritates our best in-laws:
A calm, accumulated family feeling
That we survive though other clans go reeling,—
A sentiment that will annoy your wife,
But buttress you against the stress of life;
A doctrine not dependent on a name
Or the accoutrements of transient fame,
But adequacy quietly achieved,—

The right to live from those who rightly lived:
Farmers and judges, soldiers and professors,
Never the dispossessed or great possessors;
Avoiding, on the one hand, county farms,
And, on the other, bogus coats of arms.
In short, my dear, fail not to be a snob
To wealth ungoverned or ungoverned mob,
And be the one American whose veins
Can prove no pulsing out of Charlemagne's.

How many honoured names have played the fool
In social registers at boarding school,
Where youngsters form a library restricted
To lists of the elect and unelected;
A Calvinistic Judgment Day on earth,
Predestined by unworthy money's worth;
To sneer so natural, so unbent to laugh,
And calf love guided by the golden calf.
Soap-box or scented soap; the two extremes
Make nightmares of our democratic dreams.
That choice you must avoid; ay, there's the rub—
To join, but not exemplify, a club;
Or live on Grub Street and not be a grub.

I can not hope for you long years of peace;
Frail flies the halcyon from the shores of Greece.

Not long the tranquil sunlight, and not long
The sailors' cheerful chant, the pastoral song.
See, the waves turn to lead; the sun goes under
Thick looming cumuli alive with thunder.
For one false moment Nature holds its breath,
Then heights fall down, depths rise up from beneath.
In vain to furl the sail or guess the stars;
The storm that rends the hull snaps off the spars;
The rudder steers no course,—one aimless arc
And then the final dive into the dark.
Ships wood or steel, their captains fools or sages,
So they go, so men go, so go the ages.
And yet you still may read on empty graves
Where those should sleep who sleep beneath the
    waves:
"Sail thou! for even as we perished, we
Saw other ships sail on across the sea."
Let pale Lucretius from his sheltered coast
Rejoice in safety while the brave are lost.
Afraid of living as he feared the ocean,
He drank at last a love-inflaming potion
That killed Lucretius with his first emotion.

Dear son, if in this *pater filio*
I dare not gild the evils that I know,
Be not alarmed. Most generations think

Their world is trembling on the final brink.
My generation, nurtured on the pleasant
Illusion of a static world—that wasn't—
Woke with a start, both world and vision gone;
Yet better waking so, than dreaming on.
I'd gladly lap you in a Lydian theme,
But stronger musics penetrate the dream,
The pulsing drum, the bugle, and the blast
That overthrows all ivory towers at last.
Go not to war except in your own heart,
To quell unreason and tear greed apart.
Take up your sword to guard that quiet gate
Against blind hatred in a world of hate.
Go not to war,—there's not a cause that gives
Life to the soldier who no longer lives.
No eloquence in how enduring stone
Makes unknown soldiers, to the future, known.
Go not to war! if Peace has lost her war
There is no other thing worth fighting for.
That dreamy Pharaoh who, beside the Nile,
Beheld the outstretched hands of morning smile;
When courier on courier cried for aid,
Let empires crumble, and was not afraid.
"Assyria mocks your honour. Babylon
Flames in revolt; your provinces are gone!
Send out your armies to maintain your pride."

The armies were not sent; the empire died.
Who cares to what dead sovereign it gives
Its dead allegiance? King Akhnaten lives!

Though life is perilous with war and wrack,
With fears that linger, loves that come not back;
Out of the fretted sea in after years
The slow-grown coral isle of joy appears.
I can not envy you your coming teens
That seize on life, not knowing what it means.
The twenties such dogmatic japes commit
As later strain apologetic wit.
The thirties labour, pucker-browed with fear
Of mornings after and a lame career.
But forty-one,—your mother for a wife,
You for a son,—establishes a life.
You in your first, I in my fifth, decade,
Perhaps are happiest when all is said.
But happiness so different, as to smother
Hopes of translating either to the other.
Yours is that rainbow web so finely spun
To catch the golden motes that dust the sun,
Floating along light air, a filmy skein
Torn by one gust or shattered by the rain.
But how shall I, to whom that joy is lost,
In memory's dull mirror find its ghost?

And how shall you, who know the shining thing,
Snare what is nothing if not on the wing?
Like gold, it goes as soon as you have felt it;
Time is the *aqua regia* to melt it,—
Time that brings love and debts and daily shaving;
So spend the gold that vanishes with saving.

Now the November dusk is closing in,
The ink grows thick, the inspiration thin.
Away with you! don't read across my shoulder,
For that is rude; and this waits till you're older.
Time for your music lesson! Every key
Gleams like a tooth awaiting dentistry.
Be merciful, be careful, for my sake.
'Tis not piano keys, but ears that ache.
Well-played, enrapt musician! I at nine
Had surely bungled that melodic line.
So in all things I tried, may you succeed,—
But pray be not a poet. O give heed
To filial conscience, lest my poet's name
Be mere parental adjunct to your fame.
Yet if you were my rival, I should be
Content though lost in your biography.
Play on, and happiness attend your song,
Sweet be its cadence, and its echoes, long.

A LETTER TO
QUEEN NEFERTITI

Exquisite Nefertiti, blossom furled
In secret fragrance from a wind-swept world,
Sweet are your lips, but closed to revelation;
Wide are your eyes, but lost in meditation;
Beauty you are incarnate, but as far
From invocation as a wandering star.
You are not dead, a pulse moves in the veins
High in that lovely neck, a flush remains
From lost desire along your modeled cheek,
And the lips almost speak but do not speak.
Triumphant always, always crowned, the Nile
Curved in the furtive wisdom of your smile,
You live when gods and goddesses are gone
Graven in thoughts stranger than graven stone.

Your lord, Akhnaten, who defied the priests,
And slew the gods, the half-men, the half-beasts;
Invited Egypt's doom and that mad curse
Which should pursue him through the universe.
Surely no solitary zeal could fire
Deeds so heroic with result so dire;
You were his heart-beat, you his secret breath,
That changed his shy misgivings into faith.

How young you were, young sacrificial pair,
Driving the deities of earth and air
Before you in long columns of despair.
Ra, the All-father, pilot of the Sun,
In whose eternity all days are one,—
The turquoise sycamores no more invite
His launching of the dawn from shores of night.
Thoth gravely folds his tablets and departs,
Anubis guards no more the quiet hearts
That sleep in painted tombs; his jackal-head
Withdrawn in death from vigil of the dead.
Let Horus end his endless strife with Set;
Sad Isis, now forgotten, can forget;
Her beautiful Osiris will not rise
For all her son's wild vengeance and her cries.
Farewell to magic! let the sun come forth
Crowned with the double crown of South and North.

But in their city, though the gods were gone,
Three thousand years of incense smouldered on;
All Thebes too smoky with their burnt-out law
To see the One God whom Akhnaten saw.
Farewell to Thebes! lost citadel of lies,—
Let the new city of the Truth arise.
Now lingers still in your uplifted face
That dream of light and uncorrupted space:

The City-of-the-Wide-Horizon! There
The happy gave no sacrifice but prayer.
And prayer itself more like a lovers' meeting,—
To everlasting God, eternal greeting.
For living men, no longer for the dead,
Arcades of painted lotus columns spread
Their cool, delicious gloom of shadow, stirred
By murmuring waters, hidden and half-heard.
Amid the marble-margined lake, swift oars
Digging bright water, flung up jets of stars;
They moved to rhythms strong and yet unstrained
In a new world; alas, still to be gained.

All Egypt quickened to the sunlit news
Of streets at peace, untempled avenues,
Of paintings strange as truth, and statues giving
New beauty to the beauty of the living.
And in the morning sun, the wondering King
Embraced you as he bade his people sing;
And merrily they sang, and merrily
The lake reëchoed when the King rowed by.

The tall primeval gods your lord had doomed,
Lay full-length in the cliffs of dark entombed;
Their granite coffins sealed with painted eyes
Blind with the dust of thirty centuries.

63 ·

But as a thought of things we dare not name,
Passing across the mind in waves of shame,
Is banished to the soul's Lethean streams
Only to rise in sleep and taint our dreams,
So in that cavern where the gods lay dead
Surely some creature stirred, some word was said.
A ghost of motion, phantom of a sigh,
And breath regained by one who could not die.
High in the upper world your harps played on,
Your daughters danced in courtyards of the sun,
Neferiu, the Queen of Babylon,
And that dark sister, who some time should reign
In Egypt with Egyptian gods again.
But underground, emboldened by one breath
Of lifeless air, one goddess stirred in death;
Sekhmet, the lion-headed queen of war,
Knew well the shield of destiny she bore,
She the immortal, she the deathless hate,
Who shall outlive all things but love and fate.

The granite coffin lid heaves up a crack,
Two mad eyes glitter, as they pierce the black.
Slowly the goddess writhes from the embrace
Of heavy death, and drops with cat-like grace
To the cold tiles of darkness, while her sight
Widens its yellow orbit to the night.

Whining and purring, she surveys the hosts
Of deity, fogged by their hovering ghosts.
And rising up she moves with privy smile
Among the dead down that tremendous aisle.
With velvet tap she touches one by one
The stones, and something stirs beneath the stone.
"My darlings, death is brief for queens of war.
I have arisen; you shall rise once more.
You shall return victorious in my train
And in a world laid waste be gods again.
The heretic of Egypt shall bow down
To lay before my feet his double crown.
Who can resist my charm?—Let him resist,
And death shall kiss the lips that love has kissed."

From every province of the Empire came
Wild messengers fleeter than forest flame.
"A phantom goddess with a lion's head
Wanders through Asia, raising up the dead.
Dead hatreds sweep your provinces, dead hands
Reach for their swords through all your subject
    lands.
From every rock and tree her face appears.
The lonely traveler at midnight hears
A whisper from the desert, 'Do you bring
Tribute to Egypt? What of Egypt's King?

Where are his armies? Do your kings enjoy
Subjection to a heretic, a boy?' "
Akhnaten smiled, "Then let the tribute cease.
Gold as the sunlight is the gold of peace."
The City-of-the-Wide-Horizon rang
No longer with the songs that lovers sang,
But with the lamentations, first of doubt,
And then of frenzy, in one desperate shout.
"Rebellion sweeps like fire through withered grass.
Onrushing spears in blazing tumult pass
From city unto city. I alone
Escaped to bring these tidings to your throne."
"Not one Egyptian shall go forth. Not one."

And you, Queen Nefertiti, as you heard
The first lament, the last defiant word,
Did you implore your lord, as others would
To yield the greater to the lesser good?
Did you, as women do the wide world over,
Beg worldly grants from an unworldly lover?
And did you whisper in the night, "My lord,
Send but one army, but unsheath one sword,
And all your rebel provinces will quail
Before your might that Truth may still prevail.
Must we give up this lovely holiday
Of life and let the Empire fall away?

Surely my love, surely one show of force
Could not divert Peace from its fated course."
Never! no woman's wisdom and no guile
Lurk in the strange half-turning of your smile,
But that sustaining peace which held his faith
Immaculate until the gates of death;
When, with the loneliest of human cries,
Amid the painted flowers and butterflies,
He fell full-length; his heart a stone of doubt
In frozen blood. And so the Sun went out.

And so the gods in ancient Thebes once more
Took calm possession in the wake of war.
Thoth on his tablets faithfully inscribed:
"Gods take on life again when Death is bribed."
Anubis from his shadowy altar gave
His benediction to the reeking grave.
Sweet Isis, *Iside Invicte*, tall
In triumph, dreamed of Rome and Roman Gaul.
But Sekhmet smiled. She need not vaunt her
      name
Who in all lands and ages is the same.
Your daughter's lord, the king Tut-ankh-amen,
Summoned the priests, sent armies forth again,
Won back the Empire King Akhnaten spurned,
And all things to their wonted course returned.

Small wonder that the priests, for his reward,
Sealed up that laughably majestic hoard
Which holds his spirit weighted to this day,
The dupe of time, to vulgar eyes the prey.
Small wonder that their maledictions dinned
Akhnaten's ashes down a friendless wind,—
The Heretic, the Outlaw; let them chase
His twittering spirit into empty space.
How had they understood—if they had known!—
That flight of the alone to the Alone?
The City-of-the-Wide-Horizon, brought
To loneliness, to ruin, and to naught,
Sank under ripples of the sand,—so soon
Dawn died in the long desert afternoon,
Where ebbing centuries for ever keep
The bright dream buried under tides of sleep.

Young widowed Queen, in whose prophetic eyes
The happiness, but not the rapture, dies,
Surely the God you worshipped as the One
Resolved your spirit homeward to the sun.
Surely you were not left, half-blind, to grope
Your aimless way amid the shards of hope;
In streets of rubbish, courtyards of decay,
Where once you sang the sunrise hours away,—
Surely? I can not know. Perhaps I pray.

Fickle as victory, December sends
False April northward on the winter winds;
Oblivious to inevitable snow
I watch brief sunlight on your statue glow.
Brief interlude of radiance,—though it pass,
And nightfall splinter frost on withered grass,
Still the false Aprils quicken us, as bright
Forerunners swift with tidings of the light.
This is the hint of one who loves to dwell
Within the heart; who never says farewell
To you, or to Akhnaten, or the best
That man has known when he has bravely guessed.
This is the voice that in the end shall sing
In cities of horizons wide with spring.

A NOTE ON THE TYPE IN WHICH
THIS BOOK IS SET

Pierre Simon Fournier (le jeune), who designed the type from which that used in this book is adapted, was both an originator and a collector of types. His services to the art of printing were his design of letters, his creation of ornaments and initials, and his standardization of type sizes. His types are old style in character and sharply cut. In 1764 and 1768 he published his "Manuel Typographique," a treatise on the history of French types and printing, on type-founding in all its details, and on what many consider his most important contribution to typography — the measurement of type by the point system (1 point now equals $\frac{1}{72}$ inch).

COMPOSED, PRINTED, AND BOUND BY
The Plimpton Press, NORWOOD, MASS.
PAPER MADE BY
S. D. Warren Co., BOSTON

Date Due

NO 19 82